ANIMALS IN DANGER!

Chimpanzees

Nancy Dickmann

BROWN BEAR BOOKS

Published by Brown Bear Books Ltd
4877 N. Circulo Bujia
Tucson, AZ 85718
USA

and

Unit 1/D, Leroy House
436 Essex Rd
London N1 3QP
UK

© 2019 Brown Bear Books Ltd

ISBN 978-1-78121-441-1 (library bound)
ISBN 978-1-78121-463-3 (paperback)

Library of Congress Cataloging-in-Publication
Data available on request

Text: Nancy Dickmann
Designer: Supriya Sahai
Design Manager: Keith Davis
Picture Researcher: Laila Torsun
Editorial Director: Lindsey Lowe
Children's Publisher: Anne O'Daly

Manufactured in the United States of America
CPSIA compliance information: Batch#AG/5623

Picture Credits
The photographs in this book are used by
permission and through the courtesy of:

Front Cover: iStock: guenterguni.
Ardea: Michael Nuegebauer 20; Dreamstime:
Hel080808 16–17, Mark Higgins 12; FLPA: Franz
Lanting 12–13; iStock: Afimages 14–15, Robert
Ford 14, guenterguni, 1, justhavealook 21,
kiamsoon 10, Rolling Earth 4, USO 18–19,
Vladimir Vladimirov 8–9; NaturePL: Suzi Eszterhas
18, Arup Shah 8; Shutterstock: Nick Biemans 5,
Sam DCruz 6–7, Serge Hussar 16, Sergey
Uryadnikov 10–11.

All other artwork and photography
© Brown Bear Books.

t-top, r-right, l-left, c-center, b-bottom

Brown Bear Books has made every attempt
to contact the copyright holder. If you have
any information please contact:
licensing@brownbearbooks.co.uk

Websites
The website addresses in this book were valid
at the time of going to press. However, it is
possible that contents or addresses may
change following publication of this book.
No responsibility for any such changes can
be accepted by the author or the publisher.
Readers should be supervised when they
access the Internet.

Words in **bold** appear in the Useful Words
on page 23.

Contents

What Are Chimpanzees?

Chimpanzees are related to gorillas and monkeys. We often call them "chimps." Chimps belong to a group called **primates**. Humans are primates, too.

Chimps are our closest living relatives.

Chimps are smaller than humans. But they are strong. They usually walk on all fours. They can also walk on two legs.

5

Habitats and Food

A **habitat** is the place where an animal lives. Chimps live in **tropical forests**. They live in Africa. Chimps are built for forest life. Their arms are long and strong. They swing between branches.

The places where chimps live are warm and wet.

Africa

Atlantic Ocean

Indian Ocean

WOW!

Chimps make nests in trees for sleeping. The nests are made from leaves and branches.

Chimps mostly eat plants. They like fruit best. They also eat leaves, flowers, and roots. Sometimes they hunt monkeys and other small animals.

Using Tools

Chimps use simple tools. They use stones or branches to crack nuts. They put the nut on a hard surface. Then they hit it with a stone.

A skilled chimp can crack 100 nuts in a day.

Chimps use sticks as tools. They scoop honey
out of beehives. They also catch **termites**.
They poke the stick into the insects' nest.
When they pull it out, they eat the insects on it.

How Chimps Communicate

Chimps live in groups. They communicate with each other. They use different calls. Some calls warn about danger. Others tell where food is.

A grin can mean that a chimp is frightened.

WOW!

A chimp called Washoe learned sign language. She could "talk" to humans.

Chimps groom each other's fur.

They pick out mud and insects.

This can be a way of making friends.

Baby Chimpanzees

A baby chimp is small and helpless.
It clings to its mother's fur. The mother feeds
her baby on milk. Soon she teaches
it to find food. At about six months,
the baby can ride on its mother's back.

Young chimps love to play. They chase each other. They run and climb. The chimps are learning useful skills while they play.

WOW!
Older females sometimes babysit the young chimps.

Chimpanzees in Danger

Chimps are **endangered**. They are at risk of dying out completely. Lions kill some chimps. Others die of **disease**. Many die because their **habitat** is disappearing.

People cut down forests where chimps live. They grow crops on the land. They sell the wood or use it. Without the forests, chimps cannot survive.

WOW!

Chimps can catch diseases from humans. Many of them die.

Poaching

It is against the law to kill chimps.
But some people hunt them anyway.
This is called poaching. **Poachers**
eat the meat or sell it. They also sell
chimps as pets.

It is **illegal** to
catch chimps.
Poachers ignore
this law.

16

Farmers sometimes kill chimps who eat their crops. Some chimps are caught in traps set for other animals. In national parks, **rangers** protect chimps. They try to stop people killing them.

What's Next?

Scientists track chimps. They count them. They check if they are healthy. Some people rescue baby chimps whose mothers have died. Others work to protect the chimps' **habitat**.

Rescued baby chimps are cared for. Some of them will be released back into the wild.

There are less than half a million chimps left. If their habitat keeps shrinking, they might die out. People need to protect chimps.

Chimpanzee Helpers

These groups help chimps:

The International Union for Conservation of Nature (IUCN) is a group of scientists. The scientists count animals. They keep track of their numbers. They decide whether an animal is **endangered**. They say when it has gone **extinct**.

The World Wildlife Fund is a charity. It helps protect forests where chimps live.

Jane Goodall is a scientist who studies chimps. She started a charity that helps them.

Fact File

Average life span:
up to 45 years

Height: 4–5.5 feet
(1.2 –1.7 meters)

Weight: 70–130 pounds
(32–59 kilograms)

Diet: fruit, plants, meat

Groups: from 3 to 15
members. Groups can
join up to form even
larger groups.

WOW!
A group of
chimps is often
called a troop.

Try It!

Imagine that you are a scientist. You are studying a group of chimps. Make a bar graph to show their favorite fruit.

You will need:
- graph paper
- pencil
- ruler
- colored pencils

Fruit	Amount Eaten
Bananas	2 pounds
Berries	1 pound
Figs	8 pounds
Mangoes	4 pounds

1 Write "Fruit" at the bottom of the graph. Write the fruits on the line. They should be evenly spaced.

2 Along the side, write "Pounds eaten." Write in numbers from 1 to 10.

3 Look at the data in the table. For each fruit, plot the number on the graph.

4 Use the ruler to make a bar for each fruit. Color it in. Which fruit has the highest bar?

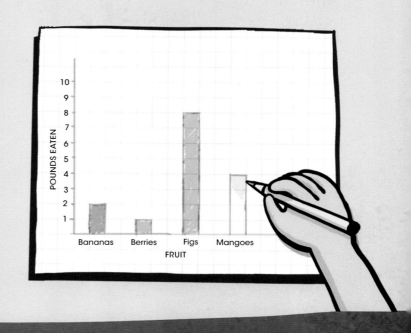

Useful Words

disease A serious illness.

endangered In danger of dying out completely so that no more are left.

extinct Having died out completely so that no more are left.

habitat The place where a plant or animal lives.

illegal Against the law.

poacher A person who hunts or traps animals when it is against the law.

primate A mammal in the group that includes humans, monkeys, and chimps.

ranger A person whose job is patrolling a park or forest to keep animals safe.

termite An insect with a pale, soft body that eats wood. Termites live in nests made of mud.

tropical forest An area in a warm part of the world where trees grow thickly.

Find Out More

Websites

www.worldwildlife.org/species/chimpanzee

janegoodall.ca/our-stories/category/great-apes/

www.nationalgeographic.com/animals/mammals/c/chimpanzee/

Books

Chimpanzees Grace Hansen, ABDO Kids, 2015

It's a Chimpanzee! Tessa Kenan, Lerner Classroom, 2017

Jane Goodall: Champion for Chimpanzees Jodie Shepherd, Children's Press, 2015

Index